POLAR ANIMALS
LIFE IN THE FREEZER

ARCTIC FOXES

by Ruth Owen

**WINDMILL
BOOKS**™

New York

Published in 2013 by Windmill Books, An Imprint of Rosen Publishing
29 East 21st Street, New York, NY 10010

Produced for Windmill by Ruby Tuesday Books Ltd
Editor for Ruby Tuesday Books Ltd: Mark J. Sachner
US Editor: Sara Antill
Designer: Emma Randall
Consultant: Dudley Wigdahl, Curator of Mammals and Birds,
Long Beach Aquarium of the Pacific, California

Photo Credits:
Cover, 1, 8–9, 9 (top), 9 (bottom right), 10 (top left), 10 (top right), 11, 13, 14 (bottom), 17, 18 (bottom), 21, 27, 28–29 © Shutterstock; 4–5, 7, 10 (bottom left), 19, 22–23, 24–25 © FLPA; 9 (center right) © Dawn Endico, Wikipedia Creative Commons; 14–15 © istockphoto; 18 (center) © Bruce McAdam, Wikipedia Creative Commons; 20 © Alamy.

Library of Congress Cataloging-in-Publication Data

Owen, Ruth, 1967–
Arctic foxes / by Ruth Owen.
    p. cm. — (Polar animals: life in the freezer)
Includes index.
ISBN 978-1-4777-0222-2 (library binding) — ISBN 978-1-4777-0231-4 (pbk.) —
ISBN 978-1-4777-0232-1 (6-pack)
1. Arctic fox—Juvenile literature. I. Title.
QL737.C22O966 2013
599.776'4—dc23
                                        2012026936

Manufactured in the United States of America

CPSIA Compliance Information: Batch # BW13WM: For Further Information contact Windmill Books, New York, New York at 1-866-478-0556

CONTENTS

FINDING FOOD IN THE FREEZER

It is an icy-cold winter day in one of the most extreme places on Earth—the **Arctic**. In this bleak, freezer-like environment, three hungry animals are on the hunt for food.

A polar bear has walked for miles (km) over the frozen surface of the Arctic Ocean. It knows there are seals in the water beneath the ice. It also knows that seals must pop up from underwater at holes in the ice to breathe. If a seal appears at a breathing hole, the bear will be ready to attack the animal. Then it will feed on the seal's fat, or blubber.

Following the giant **predator** are two arctic foxes. They know that if the bear catches a seal, there will be leftovers of seal meat, skin, and bones. Once the bear has eaten its fill of blubber, it will move on. Then the hungry foxes will feast on the remains of the bear's meal.

Feeding on polar bear leftovers is a dangerous strategy for an arctic fox because a polar bear will kill and eat the fox if it gets the chance. The fox must stay out of sight or maintain a safe distance from the bear at all times.

Polar bear

Arctic fox

5

THE WORLD OF THE ARCTIC FOX

Arctic foxes live in areas of Alaska, Canada, Greenland, Russia, Finland, Norway, and Sweden that are inside the **Arctic Circle** or are subarctic, just south of the Arctic Circle. Arctic foxes also live in Iceland.

Arctic foxes live mostly in coastal places that border the Arctic Ocean.

In the Arctic Ocean there is a vast area of permanently frozen ocean called the polar ice cap. In winter, the ocean around the ice cap freezes, too. Then the sea

WHERE ARCTIC FOXES LIVE

Pacific
Ocean

NORTH
AMERICA

Alaska

Arctic Ocean

ASIA

Canada

Russia

Polar ice cap
and sea ice
in winter

Greenland

Iceland

Norway
Sweden
Finland

Atlantic
Ocean

Arctic Circle

EUROPE

The red areas on the map show where arctic foxes live.

ice spreads to join with the coastlines of the surrounding countries.

Arctic foxes live mostly on land, but during winter they will sometimes venture out onto the frozen ocean to look for food.

Arctic foxes are Iceland's only native land **mammal**. This means they naturally live in Iceland and were not brought to the country by humans, as is the case with all the island's other land mammals.

An arctic fox on the sea ice

LIFE ON THE TUNDRA

Arctic foxes live in one of the harshest, coldest **habitats** on Earth, the Arctic **tundra**. For much of the year, the rocky land is covered with ice or snow.

No trees or other large plants with deep-growing roots can live on the tundra because the land is covered with just 3 feet (1 m) of soil. Below this soil there is nothing but **permafrost**—permanently frozen ground. Only plants with shallow roots, such as tough grasses and low-growing mosses, which can withstand the fierce Arctic winds, can survive in this habitat.

For just 50 to 60 days each year, temperatures rise during the Arctic summer. Then the ice and snow melt and many of the tundra plants briefly burst into color. These plants produce flowers, berries, and seeds that are a welcome food source for the tundra's animals.

In winter, temperatures on the Arctic tundra may drop to -40°F (-40°C). Freezing winds can blow at up to 60 miles per hour (97 km/h).

Arctic fox

In winter, only the toughest plants can survive under the tundra snow and ice.

Arctic tundra summer plant life

Arctic poppies

Lingonberries

Cottongrass plants

MEET THE NEIGHBORS

It's hard to imagine that the inhospitable Arctic tundra could support many animals. However, the arctic fox lives alongside many different mammals, birds, and insects. Some tundra animals are predators, while others are **prey**.

The arctic fox is both a predator and a prey animal. Small tundra creatures such as lemmings, voles, squirrels, and birds are the foxes' main prey.

The enemies of the fox are the Arctic's top predators, polar bears and wolves. These large hunters catch and eat small tundra animals, but they also hunt caribou and the huge musk oxen that roam the icy land grazing on the tundra's tough plants.

Musk oxen

Gray wolf

Lemming

To survive in
the Arctic, it's best not
to be a fussy eater.
Arctic foxes hunt for
live prey, but they are also
scavengers that will eat the
remains of a rotting carcass,
or dead body, abandoned
by another hunter.

PHYSICAL FACTS— BUILT FOR COLD

Arctic foxes are perfectly adapted to living in an extremely cold environment.

To reduce the amount of heat that is lost from the surface of their bodies, they have small bodies. Their legs and muzzles are much shorter than those of red foxes, which live in warmer habitats. Arctic foxes do not have long, pointed ears like their red fox cousins, but have short, more rounded ears with far less surface area.

From the tips of their noses to their bottoms, adult arctic foxes can measure 18 to 27 inches (46–69 cm). They can weigh as little as 6 pounds (2.7 kg) or as much as 17 pounds (7.7 kg).

Arctic foxes have fur on the soles of their paws. This fur helps them grip onto slippery ice and snow as they walk and run.

Short ears

Short muzzle

Small body

In the wild, arctic foxes usually live for between three and six years.

13

WRAPPED UP WARM

The most outstanding feature of an arctic fox is its stunning, thick, white fur coat.

The coat is so dense and insulating that an arctic fox will not feel cold even in temperatures below −40°F (−40°C). An arctic fox's fur gives the animal better protection against the cold than any other mammal that scientists have ever studied.

The fox's tail, which is known as a "brush," is also covered with thick fur. When the fox is in an open place and freezing winds or blizzards begin to blow, the fox hunkers down on the ground and curls its tail around its face like a thick scarf.

Some arctic foxes have grayish coats.

An arctic fox's bushy tail is around 13 inches (33 cm) long.

A COAT FOR ALL SEASONS

In winter, most arctic foxes have a white coat, but some have fur that is more grayish or bluish-white.

The fur doesn't only keep the foxes warm. The colors of their coats are also good **camouflage** against the snow and ice. This helps the foxes stay hidden from their predators.

In April, arctic foxes begin to shed, or lose, their winter coats. By summer, they have thin coats of brown or grayish-brown fur. This color scheme helps the foxes blend into the grays and browns of the rocky summer tundra. A thinner coat also prevents the foxes from overheating when the temperature rises in summer.

As snow and cold weather approach again in September, arctic foxes begin to regrow their thick white or bluish-white winter coats.

An arctic fox's winter and summer looks are so different that it's difficult to see that it is the same type of animal. In winter, the foxes look short and chubby, while in summer they look skinny and long-legged.

Whether it's winter or summer, an arctic fox always has the right thing to wear to make sure predators can't see it!

This arctic fox uses camouflage in the snow.

FOX FOOD

Arctic foxes are **omnivores**. They hunt and scavenge for meat and will also **forage** for other types of food.

Arctic foxes eat fish, insects, berries, and even the waste of other animals.

Foxes that live close to the seashore take eggs and chicks from ground-nesting birds such as arctic terns and snow geese. They will also catch and kill adult seabirds.

Arctic tern eggs in a ground nest

An arctic tern defending its nest

Stealing from the nests of arctic terns can be dangerous for arctic foxes. The birds aggressively defend their nests by dive-bombing predators and stabbing them with their pointed beaks!

Guillemots are seabirds that nest on high cliffs. When it's time for the guillemot chicks to leave their nests, the little birds open their wings and try to glide out to the ocean. Most do not make it. They crash onto the beaches below, where hungry arctic foxes are waiting to catch as many chicks as possible!

An arctic fox pup eating a seabird

HUNTING SKILLS

Adult arctic foxes move from place to place looking for food. A fox might hunt and forage for food alone, or get together with other foxes to search for food in a group.

An arctic fox pouncing on prey beneath the snow

In winter, the foxes' prey, such as lemmings and voles, are hidden under thick snow. This isn't a problem for the fox. This skillful hunter uses its excellent sense of hearing to listen for the little animals scurrying around in the tunnels they dig beneath the snow. Once the fox precisely locates its victim, it attacks. The fox leaps up into the air and pounces hard, breaking through the snow to grab the little animal before it knows what has happened.

To survive the Arctic winter when food is scarce, arctic foxes store extra food in their dens during the summer. They hide spare food under rocks or bury it in the cold ground. It's a little like having a deep freezer!

A fox digging in the snow to find its prey

ARCTIC FOX DENS

When arctic foxes reach adulthood, they find a partner, or **mate**. The fox pair usually stays together for life. The foxes make homes called dens where they live together and raise their young.

Arctic foxes may dig a den in a mound of soil out on the open tundra. They may also dig dens under piles of rocks below cliffs.

A den may have up to eight different entrances. Inside the den are tunnels that lead to small underground rooms where the foxes sleep. The rooms and tunnels of the den may spread over an area that is up to 300 square feet (30 m/sq).

An arctic fox pair may build and use several different dens. Some dens are passed down from generation to generation and may be used for over 100 years.

A pair of arctic foxes stand outside their den. The entrance is hidden beneath rocks.

ARCTIC FOX PUPS

An arctic fox pair may raise two **litters** of pups each summer. They will mate for the first time around March or April, and the pups are born seven to eight weeks later.

The female arctic fox gives birth to a litter of around five pups. A litter may be much larger, however, with 15 to 20 pups born at one time!

The female fox feeds the pups with milk from her body. When the pups are around three weeks old, they begin to spend some time outside the den.

A few weeks after the first litter of pups is born, the foxes mate again, and a second litter is born in July or August.

Female arctic fox

A litter of arctic fox pups may be a mixture of colors. Some may have white or gray fur, while their brothers and sisters may have brown or grayish-brown fur.

Arctic fox pups feeding from their mother

FOX FAMILY LIFE

Arctic fox pups begin to eat meat, which their parents bring to them, when they are around three weeks old.

By the time the pups are about six weeks old, they are fully weaned, which means they no longer drink milk and only eat adult foods.

The parent foxes begin to teach their pups how to hunt and forage, and by the time the pups are three months old, they spend time away from the den and are able to catch and find their own food.

Most pups leave their parents and go off to live on their own when they are around 10 months old. Sometimes a young fox will stay with its parents for a year or more, though. When its parents have new babies the following summer, the one-year-old fox helps care for its new brothers and sisters by bringing them food.

Many young foxes die before they are a year old. Some are killed by predators, while many die because there is too much competition for food in years when lemming or vole numbers are low. Surviving their first winter, when food is scarce, can also be tough for youngsters.

An arctic fox pup at the entrance to its family's den

ARCTIC FOXES AND HUMANS

In many parts of the Arctic, native people have hunted arctic foxes for generations.

The foxes' thick fur is an important source of income for many native communities. Hunters shoot arctic foxes and catch them in traps.

Arctic foxes are also bred and raised on fur farms to be killed for their coats. For many people, this is unacceptable. Arctic foxes are smart animals designed by nature to roam and hunt and forage. Foxes on farms live in small cages and are usually killed at just seven months old so their fur can be harvested.

Thankfully, in most parts of the Arctic the hunting of wild arctic foxes has not affected their numbers. The foxes are able to breed quickly and rebuild their numbers, so hunting has not endangered them for the future. Today, scientists estimate that there are several hundred thousand arctic foxes living wild on the icy Arctic tundra, and surviving life in the freezer.

Millions of arctic foxes and other wild animals are bred every year to supply the fur industry. While some countries, such as the United Kingdom, Austria, and Switzerland, have banned fur farming, it is still allowed in the United States and many other parts of the world.

GLOSSARY

Arctic (ARK-tik)
The northernmost area on Earth, which includes northern parts of Europe, Asia, and North America, the Arctic Ocean, the polar ice cap, and the North Pole.

Arctic Circle
(ARK-tik SIR-kul)
One of the major imaginary circles, called circles of latitude, that divide maps and globes of the Earth into different regions. Everything north of the Arctic Circle is called the Arctic.

camouflage
(KA-muh-flahj)
Hiding or blending into one's background. An animal's fur or skin color or pattern can camouflage it against its background.

forage (FOR-ij)
To move from place to place looking for food.

habitat (HA-buh-tat)
The place where an animal or plant normally lives. A habitat may be a rain forest, the ocean, or a backyard.

litter (LIH-ter)
A group of baby animals all born to the same mother at the same time.

mammal (MA-mul)
A warm-blooded animal that has a backbone and usually has hair, breathes air, and feeds milk to its young.

mate (MAYT)
An animal's partner that it produces young with. Also, when a male and female come together in order to have young.

omnivore (OM-nih-vawr)
An animal that eats both plants and meat, or fish.

permafrost (PUR-muh-frost)
A layer of soil below the surface that is always frozen.

predator (PREH-duh-ter)
An animal that hunts and kills other animals for food.

prey (PRAY)
An animal that is hunted by another animal as food.

scavenger (SKA-ven-jur)
An animal that feeds on dead animals, other animals' leftovers, or sometimes on trash.

tundra (TUN-druh)
A rocky, treeless, boggy landscape of low-growing plants. Below the surface is a layer of permanently frozen soil called permafrost.

Websites

For web resources related to the subject of this book, go to: www.windmillbooks.com/weblinks and select this book's title.

READ MORE

Marsico, Katie. *Arctic Fox.* Day in the Life: Polar Animals. Chicago: Heinemann-Raintree, 2012.

Person, Stephen. *Arctic Fox: Very Cool!.* Uncommon Animals. New York: Bearport Publishing, 2009.

Sisk, Maeve. *Arctic Foxes.* Animals That Live in the Tundra. New York: Gareth Stevens, 2011.

INDEX